Heaven Starts Here

WHAT NOW?

Heaven Starts Here

WHAT NOW?
AN AFTER TRANSITION GUIDE

YASMEEN FATIMAH, RN

Charleston, SC
www.PalmettoPublishing.com

Heaven Starts Here: What Now?

Copyright © 2023 by Yasmeen Fatimah, RN

All rights reserved

No portion of this book may be reproduced, stored in a retrieval system, or transmitted in any form by any means–electronic, mechanical, photocopy, recording, or other–except for brief quotations in printed reviews, without prior permission of the author.

First Edition

Paperback ISBN: 979-8-8229-2012-5
eBook ISBN: 979-8-8229-2013-2

Dedication

This book is dedicated to all those who were
gracious enough to share their own glimpses with me
so that I might share them with you.
May you be comforted and encouraged. . .

Table of Contents

A New Lens 1

My Journey 5

Immediately After 11

After the Dust Settles… 14

Keep Going 20

Glimpses 24

Just on the other side… 30

Personal Glimpses 31

About the Author 35

A New Lens

The last few years have brought about a global shift in what has been considered normal. There have been massive losses across the world, bringing about a whole new collective consciousness of grief. Grief can be defined as experiencing deep sorrow caused by loss. This can be attributed to loss of any kind. Most grief can be attributed to the loss of a loved one. Grief is normal to experience when loss occurs. I would venture to say it is necessary to process the new reality of the absence that one feels following a loss. Not fully experiencing the grief process can render great suffering for a very long time, even the span of a lifetime. If you are reading this, then it's likely that you've recently lost a loved one. Things may still be a bit surreal for you. Perhaps you're still trying to navigate through the fog of it all. The first thing to do is to allow yourself to feel. Whatever you're feeling is ok. Anger, frustration, sadness. All these emotions are likely present and possibly magnified many times anything you've ever felt. Even if it's numbness. *Death* feels final. There are no do-overs, no more chances to do things that you may want to do or say things that you wish you might've said. That's why it's so painful when we lose someone. My hope is that this guide will shed new light on the experience and remind you that death is not the end but merely an interval.

We are all spiritual beings, having a human experience of pure love and pure consciousness derived from the one who created all there is and all that ever will be. On my own personal journey of loss and the realization of self, I've discovered that *Heaven Starts Here*. It is stated in the Gospels of Luke and Matthew that we should not be looking anywhere for Heaven, because "the kingdom of heaven is among us." Within us. Therefore, there is no end, just transition into the unknown. Our spirits are pure energy and, therefore, can never be destroyed. My prayer in writing this is that it reaches those who have ears and hearts to hear, that there is an innate knowing, and that what you are reading just serves as confirmation. No matter what your core beliefs are, if you have experienced a loved one's transition and you had the privilege to experience the journey up close, you know this to be true.

The loss of a loved one is arguably the most difficult thing that we will experience in our lives. It is also the one experience that we will all have unless we ourselves transition prior to losing someone close to us. The first few weeks following someone's transition can feel unreal. You may feel like you're in a fog. The nature of the transition weighs on how one experiences, copes, and processes grief. A loved one transitioning following a battle with an illness is going to have a different effect on our consciousness than that of a loved one transitioning suddenly and unexpectedly. While most of you reading this will have experienced an expected loss following the illness of a loved one or the natural transition of an elderly loved one, some may have experienced unexpected loss when someone passes suddenly. No matter the nature of your loved one's transition, there will still be a void. It could even feel like a literal hole in your heart. My goal is to offer a different perspective on death and dying and the loss felt during these times—to offer love and light that will hopefully fill the space created by your loved one's physical absence. I have experienced my share of loss and transition of loved ones. I've learned a great deal from the experience of the initial loss and of evolving into the new normal of their physical absence.

Allow me to introduce a term that you may not be familiar with: *kensho*. Kensho is a Japanese term derived from the Zen tradition. Ken means *seeing*; sho, means *nature* or *essence*. Kensho ultimately means *seeing one's true nature*. A *kensho moment* is one in which you experience temporary pain that drives personal growth. The loss of a loved one is certainly considered a kensho moment. This experience, like every other painful experience that we will encounter during this human experience, is base metal, if you will. We have the power to transmute that experience, no matter how bad it feels, into something beautiful. Like the alchemist turns base metal into gold. My hope is that this book will help you in the processing of this experience and, thereby, arrive at a manageable space and know that, in our true essence and oneness, there is never any separation and, therefore, no loss. And I hope that the book may even help you to ultimately see the collateral beauty of it all.

My Journey

The year 2017 was particularly rough. I experienced the transition of my mother, following her long battle with a lung disease. It was very difficult to watch her going through that—to see her become more and more frail and unable to function as she normally would. You don't want to see your loved one's suffering. You pray for a miracle or what you think that would look like. I worked with a doctor in a hospice unit who I heard say to a family, "God does grant miracles. But it wouldn't be a miracle if everyone got one." I know I've shared that with numerous families, and for some it was consoling. While I have a different perspective on miracles now, there's something about bringing people back into the here and now—the present moment—that provides a sense of peace. I think that my knowing and experience helped me deal with my mother's transition. Though it did not make it easier, the knowing allowed me to be in the moment and accept what was happening. Therefore, I could simply focus on what mattered: love. Being love and loving her the best I knew how at the time. I now know that this has all been miraculous; our very being and existence is that: a miracle. In that knowing gratitude is felt and can be expressed from inside of us no matter what the outer circumstances look like. We can truly experience Heaven wherever we are and no matter what's taking place.

Traditionally when someone dies, people come to your home and sit around and ask, "How are you?" I knew I had no desire to do that. I told my godmother that I just wanted to go to bed. She let everyone know to give me some time. The weeks leading up to my mother's death were physically exhausting. I was still working my two jobs and tending to four children and their needs—all while processing what was happening. I had great support from friends and family. But this was my journey, and honestly no matter what, no one else would experience this the way that I was. Once my mother transitioned, I was numb. I had cried for months leading up to this. I had had numerous scares, thinking something had happened to her when she didn't answer my calls, only to find when I arrived at her home that she just hadn't heard the phone, and she was sitting on her bed, enjoying eating her chicken. I was always frustrated and relieved in those moments. I had lived and imagined the moment when she wouldn't be ok, countless times. So now I just wanted to lie down in my bed and feel whatever would come. I got home to my quiet empty house. As soon as I settled in my bed, I heard my mother's voice: "Snoop?" Writing that just now made me chuckle. That was my nickname that only she called me. I remember distinctly saying, "I'm not ready." I wasn't afraid. Just not ready. And there was a calm I felt. And I went to sleep.

After my day to rest, the processions of people coming over commenced. It was very much appreciated. People mean well. Some people need the comfort of being around others during the time of loss; others don't. It is important to follow how you feel, to know what you need during that time, and to know that it's ok to say, "No thank you." It is a delicate balance. The weeks following were a blur. I know life went on. I took the kids to their activities. I was off work for a little while. The most distinct event during that time was my godmother telling me that she had planned a cruise and that she couldn't get a refund, so she would miss the funeral. I remember being sad about that but understanding. She called me a couple of days after my mom passed and said to meet her for lunch. It was her, her sister, and someone else I can't remember. More fog. I remember not wanting to go, but I pulled myself together and went anyway. She just wanted to be sure I was ok before she left for her cruise. Lunch was great. We had a great time. When we were leaving, she gave me the biggest hug, like only she could. Our last hug prior to that was right before my mom transitioned. Mom was struggling, and I was at my wits' end. I was outside getting some air, and my godmother came outside with me. I remember walking towards her, and I don't remember what I said. I don't remember what she said, I just remember that she opened her arms and hugged me so tightly while I cried.

She gave me the absolute best hugs during that most difficult time. God provides. Following our lunch we stood in the parking lot of the restaurant and laughed. She gave me another big hug. Then off we went. We chatted a few times after that, then she was off on her cruise. I got through my mom's funeral. I don't remember crying much. Everything was beautiful. My eldest son spoke and provided great memories and laughs. My aunt gave the most amazing eulogy. I don't remember much else. When my godmother got back from her cruise, she called to check on me of course. We made plans to go and clean my mother's place and pack up her things and store them until I figured out what I wanted to do with them. I remember thinking that losing my mom was hard—like this really sucks—but God gave me another mom to help me through this. I was grateful for that. The morning that we were scheduled to go clean my mom's place and have the movers come, I called my godmother to see what time she would meet me. I didn't get an answer on her cell. It wasn't unusual that she would miss a call on her cell. I tried her home phone, and one of her aunts answered. We spoke briefly, and I honestly thought nothing of the conversation. I thought I heard her say that she would have her call me back. I don't remember. I think I was just trying to process going to my mother's home and her not being there. Shortly after that call I was trying to focus on preparing for this tough day, and then my cousin called.

She said she was headed to my house. I said, "Ok. Why?" She went on to talk, and I don't know what she said, but at this point, it kind of started to register that something was wrong. I remember saying, "Just tell me." She finally said, "Ann died." I remember falling to my knees like the wind was literally knocked out of me. After that—more blur and more numbness. I had lost the two most important women in my life in the span of two weeks. My mother's death I had expected. I had experienced it numerous times before it ever happened. My godmother's death I never fathomed.

If someone told me that would happen, I wouldn't have believed them. What is this madness? What was the purpose? What now? I had none of those answers. It took me quite a while to process and adjust. Even six years later, there are still some ups and downs on this journey. Still some sad moments and the noticeable physical absence. But what comes with knowing that there is no separation and walking in unity consciousness is vaster than any physical presence that either of these important souls could have ever accomplished, restricted as they were by their earthly bodies. I miss seeing their faces, but their essence and presence supports me now in ways that were not possible in this realm. The love they gave me and the loss I felt when I thought it was gone forever brought us here to this very moment. The pain I experienced has been alchemized into something I could never have imagined. Something beautiful. What I know now is that I experienced all of this for you so that I could provide you with a road map, some comfort, and a new perspective on this most difficult journey.

Immediately After

There are always similarities that we, as humans, experience in processes that we will all go through. However, each experience is still unique. A lot of it depends on how self-aware we are and how well we know our true selves. Know that even the most spiritually enlightened or religiously grounded people have really difficult times with the loss of someone who is near and dear to them. Depending on the nature of the passing of your loved one, there may be shock, denial, guilt, and a wealth of other really uncomfortable emotions. There may be anger, blame, bargaining, and a host of unanswered questions. There may be nothing. No feeling at all initially. It is important to know that a roller coaster of emotions is normal. And yes, in some cases, feeling nothing is normal. Maybe it's been a long exhausting journey. Maybe there were some complex family dynamics that weren't resolved. Some of us have or will be called to care for aging parents or loved ones who may not have been so kind to us. They perhaps did not show up in our lives the way that we would have liked. Finding yourself in a situation like this opens up a whole new level of grieving—grieving what never was. Maybe it's anticipatory grief of what's to come. Or maybe it's a realization that it will never be what you had hoped. And now you are giving something that you were never given by this person. Maybe it is none of that, and there is still numbness. The truth remains that it is all base metal with the ability to be transmuted into something beautiful. Transformed by the strongest force in the universe into pure love. Even if it's just for you. Whatever space you are in, I encourage you to accept it. Acceptance eliminates resistance. Perhaps your loved one battled a terminal illness for years, or the journey as caregiver has just been long and lonely, and now all you feel is relief. However, in that relief you feel guilty because you're not supposed to feel relieved, right? Honestly, you're supposed to feel whatever you feel. Relief after any difficult experience is over is normal. Even if the end is death. Allow whatever feelings that *do* come to come.

Allow yourself the time and space to process the physical absence of your loved one in whatever way you need to. If you had the privilege of having support during your loved one's transition in the form of hospice care or a death doula, there will likely be bereavement support available. Utilize those resources to the fullest capacity. This is a new normal and uncharted territory. And even if you have experienced the loss of someone close to you previously, often, old wounds are opened, and grief is compounded because we didn't take the time to properly process old losses. It is important to be with your feelings. Experience them fully. Experiencing them does not mean becoming your feelings. It is important to feel the sadness, feel the anger, and observe it as it passes by, much like watching the clouds in the sky. Imagine a time that you were experiencing a rainstorm, but you could see the sun shining off in the distance. When you allow grief to come without resistance, it will go in that same manner. There may be shock during the initial loss, and that can last as long as it takes one to process. The typical time frame is a few days to a few weeks. Again, this is different for everyone. Just allow it to be what it is. Don't resist your feelings. Don't allow anyone to tell you how you should feel. This experience is yours. Reality typically sets in after your loved one is laid to rest in whatever way is decided upon by you and those closest to you.

After the Dust Settles...

After you have laid your loved one to rest, and all your friends and family who were smothering you with care and concern have settled back into their lives, reality sets in. Maybe it's been a few weeks or a few months. Your loved one's room is empty. Their side of the bed is cold. They really aren't there. There are no more doctors' appointments to keep and no more meals to prepare. There is no more worrying about if they are ok because they're not there anymore. There are no more phone calls to check. There is a void. You may be holding on to every little memory or trying your best to forget because remembering is too painful. There is no exact amount of time that will pass before the visceral pain of your loss will subside. It will be different for everyone, and a lot of that will depend on you. You may start to feel better in a few weeks. As when experiencing any pain, the body heals itself and adjusts. The suffering comes from our minds replaying the pain and, therefore, reliving it over and over again. This is not wrong or right, bad or good. It is simply the mechanism of our human form. Understanding brings about clarity, and clarity brings about change. Throughout this entire journey, I encourage you to feel. Be in the moment. I do, however, encourage you to try not to become identified with those feelings. You feel sad, yes. But you are not the sadness. You feel anger and frustration, but those are not the true essence of you. Your true essence is love. You are experiencing the physical absence of your loved one through uncomfortable emotions. Grief is simply unexpressed love.

Grief is brought about by the idea that you will no longer have the opportunity to say and do the things that you once experienced with that person. Oftentimes we are in a hurry or maybe have no choice but to get back to life as usual. Sometimes we throw ourselves back into our routine to avoid feeling. I understand. However, I cannot stress this enough: feel. Feeling is the best indicator for where you are. If you don't feel the pain, it's not likely that you'll know how much more healing needs to be done. Think of a broken bone, and even if you haven't had one, you know that if you don't allow it to properly heal you will have problems forever. Now imagine having broken your leg and not feeling the pain of it. You would think that you could walk like normal.

The only problem is that even if you weren't physically feeling that pain, you'd still be causing more damage to that unhealed break. Doing so prolongs the healing and even causes permanent damage. Pain is necessary; suffering is not. Knowing that pain has a purpose and allowing yourself to feel it will eventually bring you to a place of peace. Let me remind you that your true essence is love; so is your loved ones. And they are no longer restricted by the mind and body, so they are now love in its purest form. There is a passage in Romans 8 that says, "nothing can separate us from the love of God." In my heart of hearts, I believe this passage speaks to the oneness that we are—bound forever by light and love. There is another popular passage often quoted at funerals, and I'm paraphrasing: "To be absent from the body is to be present with God." God is love, pure love for which there is no opposite. This being the case—and again I believe in my heart of hearts that it is—to be absent from the body, to pass away and leave it behind as it was designed, ashes to ashes, dust to dust—is to be present with God.

Our true essence is once again present with God, pure love reconvened with itself, for that is what we all are. And that is what you and I are as well, although we are still in our bodies. Our loved ones have simply merged back into oneness, and we can continue to experience them in the place that they've always been and always will be—in our hearts. They are in you, beside you, and all around you. For to be absent from the body (free of any restrictions, illness, or limiting beliefs) is to be present with pure love, always and forever. And you are that. I encourage you during this time, if you're ready, to look for the little glimpses. Reminders of your loved one may be painful at first, but remembering who we really are—pure love, pure consciousness and oneness—will help you continue to feel connected to them. There is no separation. I heard it said once that when we look for our loved one where they once were, we feel their absence, but when we are able to look for them where they are now, we feel their presence. They're always there. When you're ready to receive, they will show you. It may be through a song that they loved or a phrase they would always say. Maybe a random penny in your shoe.

Remember, there is no *getting over* the physical absence of a loved one. There is only adjusting to a new normal. It is very important to feel what you are feeling. I know that people grieve differently, but it is never healthy to suppress your feelings. That is like tying a rope around a boiling pot. Eventually, it will explode. And so will you. As it is with any uncomfortable emotion, it is important to face grief. Feel it. Sadness, anger, and fear are all feelings that derive from loss and uncertainty. I've heard it said numerous times by many spiritual teachers, "Face the lion, and it will disappear; run from it, and it will chase you." The lion is all those feelings you don't allow yourself to feel. You won't ever escape them if you don't face them. They will chase you down for the rest of your life. In facing those feelings, you allow the transmuting of the sadness into a better feeling—not necessarily a great feeling, certainly not the best you've ever felt, but a better one. Take baby steps and give yourself grace. Then when you see the beautiful butterfly cross your path or observe the color purple on a flower and remember that was their favorite color, you'll be able to smile, even just a little. This will be an ongoing adjustment. As long as you keep reaching for the better feeling thought, it gets better. I promise. And you'll remember that Heaven is not some faraway place, but Heaven it is right here.

* * *

HEAVEN STARTS HERE — WHAT NOW?

About a year ago, a childhood friend lost her father. He had had a long bout with pancreatic cancer. My mother had been really good friends with him and his wife. When he passed, of course, I made plans to go to his funeral. I honestly did not desire to do so. Let's face it: funerals suck. I pulled it together to go but was still having a really hard time. I hated the idea of having to go alone. Not wanting to subject anyone else to the sadness of the day, I toughed it out and headed there. The church was in a familiar part of town. It was a beautiful day. I remember trying to focus on the sunshine and just be present. As my GPS let me know I would arrive shortly, the anxiety started to rise again. As I began to turn into the parking lot of the church, a big, beautiful monarch butterfly flew across my window. In that moment I knew my mom was right there with me — never far away at all. She reminded me that Heaven is right here among us.

* * *

Keep Going

Only you can set the gauge of time for your forward movement. There are no rules. No right or wrong. Just keep going. Keep moving forward. Some days will go by with ease. Some days it will be hard to put one foot in front of the other. Some days you will need to sit and rest and maybe even cry. Rest is necessary and crying literally flushes unneeded stress hormones and toxins from your body. So, it's ok to cry; it's ok to rest. Just don't stay there. Keep going. It is important to understand that there will always be a sense of absence of our loved one felt from our human perspective. There may even be a lapse in remembering the physical absence of people who have been intricate parts of our lives. You may reach for your phone to call them and then remember they can't answer. You may be planning an event that they would normally be a part of, and your mind will include them before reality sets in again. You're not crazy. This is completely normal. And ultimately it is a reminder of our loved one's forever presence.

Knowing that my loved ones who have passed are where they've always been—in my heart—brings much comfort. Peace. Peace that passes all understanding. Knowing that they are pure love and that so am I reminds me that we are never separate. Separation in death is just an illusion. We are all made in God's image, and God is love. We are that. Remember, as I said before, nothing can ever separate us from the love of God (you, me, them, we). All are one. There's a spiritual teacher who I often listen to by the name of Ram Dass. He told a story about a friend named Emmanual. Emmanuel was a disembodied being, according to the story. Ram Dass said that he once asked Emmanuel what it was like to die. He said that Emmanuel said that dying is perfectly safe, kind of like taking off a tight shoe. I say often that my mother supports me more now than she ever could have in her physical body. She is no longer limited by her mind and physical illness. She is boundless, formless, timeless, and limitless. Your loved one is also no longer bound, and they are all around you.

* * *

YASMEEN FATIMAH, RN

Every time I would go on a trip or vacation, I would bring souvenirs back for my mom, especially once she was sick and unable to travel. It was my own little tradition—so much of one that, even a couple of years after her passing, I found myself picking up a trinket in a gift shop that I thought she might like. Only I quickly remembered she was no longer physically there. When I first experienced that, it made me sad. But as it continued to occur, I was able to smile about the fact that I knew she would've liked that gift if I had been able to give it to her. As my awareness grows, I now know maybe those were little glimpses of her letting me know that she's always here. And that she really likes that key chain... Now I'm able to laugh a lot more and really appreciate the alchemy and collateral beauty of it all.

* * *

HEAVEN STARTS HERE — WHAT NOW?

No matter your beliefs, religious background, or lack thereof, if you have experienced loss of this magnitude, the idea of life or continued existence after death will likely bring some comfort. The following are a few stories from my personal experiences as well as a few others that I have had the privilege of hearing over the years. I've also included a few pages where you can write your own glimpses as a reminder to yourself that your loved ones are never far away.

Ironically, God always provides whether we believe it or not. Look for the glimpses. Allow this process to unfold as only it can for you. It is difficult, it is personal, and no two people will experience it the same way. However, peace can be found in the knowing that we will all experience it, whether it be the death of a loved one or our own death.

When we are able to walk in the full acceptance of knowing that *heaven starts here*, each moment is cherished and appreciated all the more. That is when the base metal, which is all uncomfortable emotion, can be transmuted into pure gold, and our true essence shines through. Therefore, we are able to experience our transitioned loved one in their true essence, pure love

Glimpses

HEAVEN STARTS HERE — WHAT NOW?

My biggest struggle, as someone who isn't religious, has been trying to wrap my head around spirits and ghosts and the idea that a departed loved one is always with you. I've never felt that undeniable presence, but still, I crave the comfort, so I find it in the little things. I feel like I see 11:11 on the clock way more often than the average person, and I take that as a message of love from John. If I'm listening to music and a few special songs play in a row, I'll feel like it's from him. My very favorite is when Cal (my son) says something or makes a face EXACTLY like John would have. Tonight, the kids and I walked the square for ice cream. We've been missing him bad. It's been two years today. I was thinking about spirituality and religion and signs and wishing I was capable of that feeling and of sensing him near — about how it's been a long two years, and I just wish I was able to hear his voice again. RIGHT THEN the young man we were passing stopped his conversation with his friend and said, "'BOUT THICK AS FUCK." This was a phrase John said to me often. #powerofprayer —A.M.

* * *

YASMEEN FATIMAH, RN

I remember being with my mom when I learned Kanye West's mother had died. I said to her, "I don't know what I would do if I ever lost you." Three years later I lost her. She died on November 4th, and her birthday was November 23rd. For years I hated November. I would prepare to be filled with sadness in that month, and that is just what I experienced—sad Novembers. As time went on, I thought, why am I choosing to be sad? My mother was not sad. Her life was not sad. Our time together was not sad. From that I learned that we do not have to choose sadness to remember our loved ones. I began to have good Novembers. If I could say anything to those who are grieving, it is to be present with your grief. Let it hurt when it hurts, but when the pain eases, let it ease. Grief is a transitory emotion. Choosing to make it permanent only debilitates our well-being, and that is never what our loved ones would want for us. —K.C.

* * *

HEAVEN STARTS HERE—WHAT NOW?

One morning about a year ago I was sitting on my floor. I had just finished my morning quiet time and meditation. As I was reflecting and thinking, contemplating some circumstances that were going on at the time, I started to scroll through Facebook. Memories popped up, and I decided to take a look. It was message that my mom had posted on my wall nine years ago, and it said, "Hey Snoopie. It's Ma, looking good. Tell my boys and MooMoo, Hi. Love y'all." Those nicknames were especially assigned to me and my daughter. Only she could call us that. She gave the best nicknames. —Y.S.

* * *

On Sunday, we were all together for a normal family gathering. We listened to my brother Timmy's favorite songs, had his favorite meal, which is Salisbury steak, and he took our dog, Cooper, for a walk. He loved Cooper, and Cooper loved him. Looking back, we actually did all of Timmy's favorite things that Sunday. The following day my brother passed away. He had suddenly become ill a little while before but seemed to be improving. He was full of life and loved sports, music, and being with his family and friends. Some time had passed, and I was thinking of him, missing him as I stood in my kitchen. Suddenly Cooper ran into the kitchen, almost abruptly right up to me, and there was a very noticeable white feather stuck to him. It is still difficult to grasp that Timmy is not here physically, the way I remember, but I know he's with us every day—it's just in another way. I'm grateful for the reminders. —C.R.

* * *

HEAVEN STARTS HERE — WHAT NOW?

On Wednesday morning I decided to go for an early morning walk. I love the stillness right before the sunrise. On my way back home, I saw a big owl just perched on the fence in front of the golf course. I immediately welled up with emotion. I'm not sure why exactly. I thought I was just overwhelmed with gratitude at that moment. I think birds are beautiful. Owls are majestic.

A few days later I was having dinner with my son. During our chat I was reminding him of Sunday dinner, and he said, "I have a funeral to go to, but I'll be there after." "Of course," I said. "Who died?" He said, "You remember Solomon, who graduated with me?" I immediately had the wave of emotion that I felt when seeing the owl a few days prior. Solomon lived around the corner from us. I realized that I was in front of his house when I saw the owl during my walk. I shared with my son, and told him I thought that Solomon was wanting us to know that he was around and ok...

My son attended the funeral and told me that it was really nice. He told me that during the services a gentleman spoke who had known Solomon since he was little. He said that, about a week after Solomon passed, an owl came a sat on his porch for a while... —C.S.

Just on the other side...

When you wake up in the morning, I won't be where you left me. I won't be where you can see. Know that I am near, close; I won't ever be far away. The pain you feel, though seemingly unbearable, is the biggest sign of all. If you look for me where I've always been, in your heart, you will find some resolve. The grief you feel in this moment is simply love unexpressed. Fear that this is the end. Fortunately for us, we are forever beings—forever one, forever love. Look for me in the quiet, in the pauses, in the gentle breeze, and in the scent in the air. When you wake up in the morning, I won't be where you left me, but I won't be very far.

Personal Glimpses

Personal Glimpses

Personal Glimpses

About the Author

Yasmeen Fatimah is a registered nurse and certified Rebirthing Doula with over a decade of specialized experience in hospice and palliative care. Her calling to provide holistic and spiritual end-of-life care led her to become a certified Death Doula, although she prefers the term Rebirthing Doula. After her own spiritual awakening, she discovered her role as an Earth Angel, possessing a deep connection to the Divine and a unique ability to communicate directly with the souls embarking on their journey beyond.

Yasmeen was born and raised in Atlanta, Georgia, and is now the mother of four amazing human beings. She had the privilege of living in Hawaii on the island of Oahu for almost ten years. That is where she discovered a love for the ocean and all its wonder, and how peaceful the water really is. On her journey she realized why her love for the water is so vast. Water is the most powerful element because it is perfectly nonresistant. In that same spirit, she has learned simply to be, and to allow things to flow like water. She believes we must make space for all things to work together as they should, and allow ourselves to be in the moment and soak it in. For, truly, the moment is all we have.

For Information on End of Life Care,
Support and Resources Contact

*Because the kingdom of Heaven is within you,
wherever you are is Heaven on Earth*

YasmeenFatimah.com

www.ingramcontent.com/pod-product-compliance
Lightning Source LLC
LaVergne TN
LVHW051926060526
838201LV00062B/4704